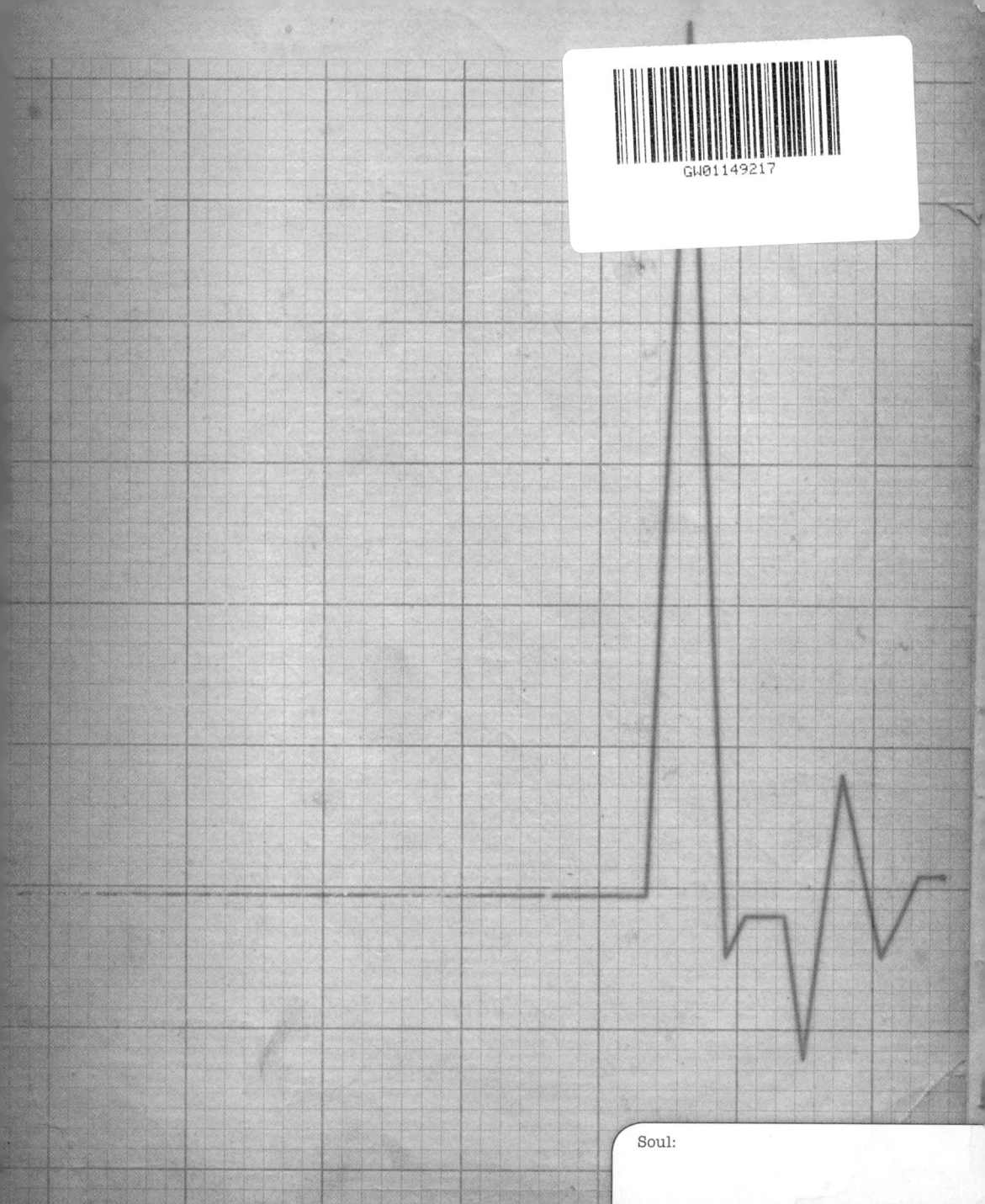

Soul:

Soul Cafe: A Guide to Spiritual Conversations
Story. Narrator. Intrigue.
© 2008 Serendipity House

Published by Serendipity House Publishers, Nashville, Tennessee

All rights reserved. No part of this work may be reproduced, stored in a retrieval system, or transmitted in any form or by any means, electronic or mechanical, including photocopying and recording, without express written permission of the publisher. Requests for permission should be addressed to Serendipity House, 117 10th Avenue North, Nashville, TN 37234.

ISBN: 978-1-5749-4421-1
Item No. 005117805

Dewey Decimal Classification: 233.5
Subject Headings: SOUL \ CHRISTIAN LIFE \ HEART--RELIGIOUS ASPECTS

Scripture quotations marked HCSB are taken from the *Holman Christian Standard Bible*®, Copyright © 1999, 2000, 2002, 2003 by Holman Bible Publishers. Used by permission.

Scriptures marked *The Message* are taken from *The Message*®. Copyright © 1993, 1994, 1995, 1996, 2000, 2001, 2002. Used by permission of NavPress Publishing Group.

Scripture quotations marked (NLT) are taken from the Holy Bible, New Living Translation, copyright © 1996. Used by permission of Tyndale House Publishers, Inc., Wheaton, IL 60189 USA. All rights reserved.

Scriptures marked NASB are taken from the *New American Standard Bible*®, Copyright © 1960, 1962, 1963, 1968, 1971, 1972, 1973, 1975, 1977, 1995 by the Lockman Foundation. Used by permission. (www.lockman.org)

To purchase Serendipity House resources:
- ORDER ONLINE www.SerendipityHouse.com
- WRITE Serendipity House, One LifeWay Plaza, Nashville, TN 37234
- FAX (615) 277-8181
- PHONE (800) 525-9563

1-800-525-9563
www.SerendipityHouse.com

Printed in the United States of America
13 12 11 10 09 08 07   1 2 3 4 5 6 7 8 9 10

PUBLISHER: Ron Keck
PROJECT MANAGER: Brian Daniel
WRITERS: Barry Cram and Brian Daniel
ART DIRECTOR: Darin Clark
COVER DESIGN: Micah Kandros
INTERIOR DESIGN: Darin Clark
EDITORIAL: Justine Scheriger and Jessie Weaver

An Invitation to Journey		4
Story. Narrator. Intrigue.		8

Conversation 1. The Eternity in Your Heart   12
Conversation 2. Psalm 51:6   18
Conversation 3. The Lounge   24
Conversation 4. Black Canvas   28
Conversation 5. Breaking Up   34
Conversation 6. Abandoned   40
Conversation 7. Bravo!   46
Conversation 8. Dr. Seuss, Grinch, Infinity   50
Conversation 9. Early Warning   54
Conversation 10. The Line   60

An Invitation to Journey

Over the course of the last few decades something strange has happened—we have forgotten the journey. Our culture has forsaken the art of the journey for a formula-driven, quick-fix destination mentality. We have forgotten how to feel, truly see, and touch. As a result, we have shied away from the wonderful yet necessary messes and made Christianity a non-mystical religion of propositional "Do this" and "Don't do that." We have lost the Story and lost touch with its Narrator.

Soul Cafe: A Guide to Spiritual Conversation is a series of open-ended conversations developed to drive you deeper into the Story God is revealing. The Soul Cafe is not a place for being comfortable or indifferent. It's personal. Penetrating. Raw. The conversation demands something from you. It isn't for the religiously refined, rather it's much better suited for the spiritual barbarian. Here's what we recommend:

- For groups ranging in number from 2–8
- Spend 10 minutes or so in each conversation prior to hooking up
- Engage the questions beforehand
- Ask God to speak into your story
- Think "point of departure"

The culture that is emerging is influenced most through dialog—art of the conversation—and technology has only made the conversation more accessible. ☙ The invitation to journey together is the impetus behind Soul Cafe: A Guide to Spiritual Conversations. A growing number of people have become engaged in spiritual conversations in the coffee shops, sandwich shops and restaurants, and cafes of our lives. Church, if it were ever exclusive to the walls of the buildings, has spilled over into the popular culture. Community has come to mean something entirely different. Because there is a need beyond curriculum, Soul Cafe has been created to serve as a guide for you as you accept the invitation into the adventure that God has extended to each of us.

The Conversation

Story. Narrator. Intrigue.

The Greek word "logos" is normally translated as "word." John 1 reveals that in the beginning was the word, or logos, and the word was God and the word was with God. But "logos" can also be translated as "story". Although this translation does not change the context, it does change the dynamic. In the beginning there was story. There has always been story. Jesus is the story. We are a part of the story.

We all know that a tree grows both up and down. As it stretches towards the sky it just as steadily digs deep. But a tree also grows out. That is, within itself are the scars from the storms it endured as sapling and the fires it withstood through the many seasons of its life. Counting the rings of a tree amounts to much more than a mathematical equation. What you are actually discovering is its story. Why certain memories remain and why you react the way you do to certain messages and environments—that's your story as it is pulled through the layers of experience. Throughout this conversation you'll feel the hard, exterior burning away.

Story. Narrator. Intrigue. includes several conversations designed to help you understand the deepest places—what the Bible refers to as your "inmost being." You will be asked to venture into dusty and rarely frequented areas and invited to peel back the many layers of your story where intrigue awaits. Throughout these conversations we'll also take questions to God—Narrator being one aspect of who He is. And like any great story, yours has a villain. You'll be asked to look back over your shoulder to find those places where your enemy, the Villain of both the Great Story of our world and smaller stories we live, has been at work since the beginning.

Remember that Soul Cafe is designed to be explored as a community. Still, it's a great idea to engage these experiences at some level before hooking up with your group. Enjoy the

THE ETERNITY IN YOUR HEART

When was the last time
you were moved deeply by
a song, movie, art, or

moment?

Think for a moment.

What was it about the event that touched you so deeply?

There was a time before time. This was a time prior to Genesis 1 or before any of our clocks—carbon or not—began recording the activities of reality. This was a time when there was harmony in the heavens between God and the angels. In this time there was apparently no creation as we now know it, but only absolute peace and fulfillment. But evil found its way into the mix. This led to betrayal, rebellion, and ultimately chaos. The Betrayer and his followers were cast out and, as Genesis opens, the Spirit broods over the void.

In the Great Narrative that has recorded what we know of our collective history we begin to see a pattern emerge. In this pattern surfaces a story with all the elements of the great stories with which we are familiar. The Epic includes a hero and a villain. And our stories include the same elements. In short, not only do we live and breathe in the epic but are also invited to fulfill a vital role in the Great Narrative that is being revealed.

The Bible tells us that God has put **eternity in our hearts** (Ecclesiastes 3:11). That is, we are born pre-wired to recognize the Great Narrative and the events associated with it when we see them played out on the screen we watch or in the music we hear or in the words we read.

What expressions of art, media, or life drive you to the greatest emotional intensity?

Why do you think we love stories? Why do you think we connect with them?

Your heart serves as something like an emotional diary or journal. It's been said that "heart" is what most people mean when they use the word "me." Your heart logs your internal story. It also tells your story.

How do you think what you feel begins to tell the story of your heart?

There are, however, times when we suppress the heart. During these times we do not want to know what is written deep inside and we hold the internal story tight. We make the heart our hostage.

How do you think you could hold your   hostage?

Conversation #2

A MAN STANDS IN LINE AT THE GROCERY STORE WITH HIS DAUGHTER. THE CASHIER, ALTHOUGH DOING HER BEST, IS HAVING TROUBLE SCANNING A PRODUCT FOR THE CUSTOMER IN FRONT OF THE MAN AND HIS DAUGHTER. EACH SECOND THAT PASSES CLEARLY BRINGS ON MORE AGITATION UNTIL IT GIVES INTO ANGER AND FINALLY LITERAL RAGE. WE CAN'T KNOW THE ACTUAL CIRCUMSTANCES SURROUNDING THE EMOTIONAL PROGRESSION. MAYBE THEY ARE RUNNING LATE IN GETTING THE DAUGHTER WHERE SHE NEEDS TO BE. MAYBE HE WORKED LATE, THROWING HIS PLANS FOR THE EVENING OFF, AND THE PRESENT SITUATION ISN'T HELPING. IT COULD BE THAT HE HAS RECENTLY LOST HIS JOB AND IS STRUGGLING TO REPLACE THE LOST INCOME.

20 ITEMS OR FEWER   **20 ITEMS OR FEWER**

5   **5**

20 Psalm 51:6

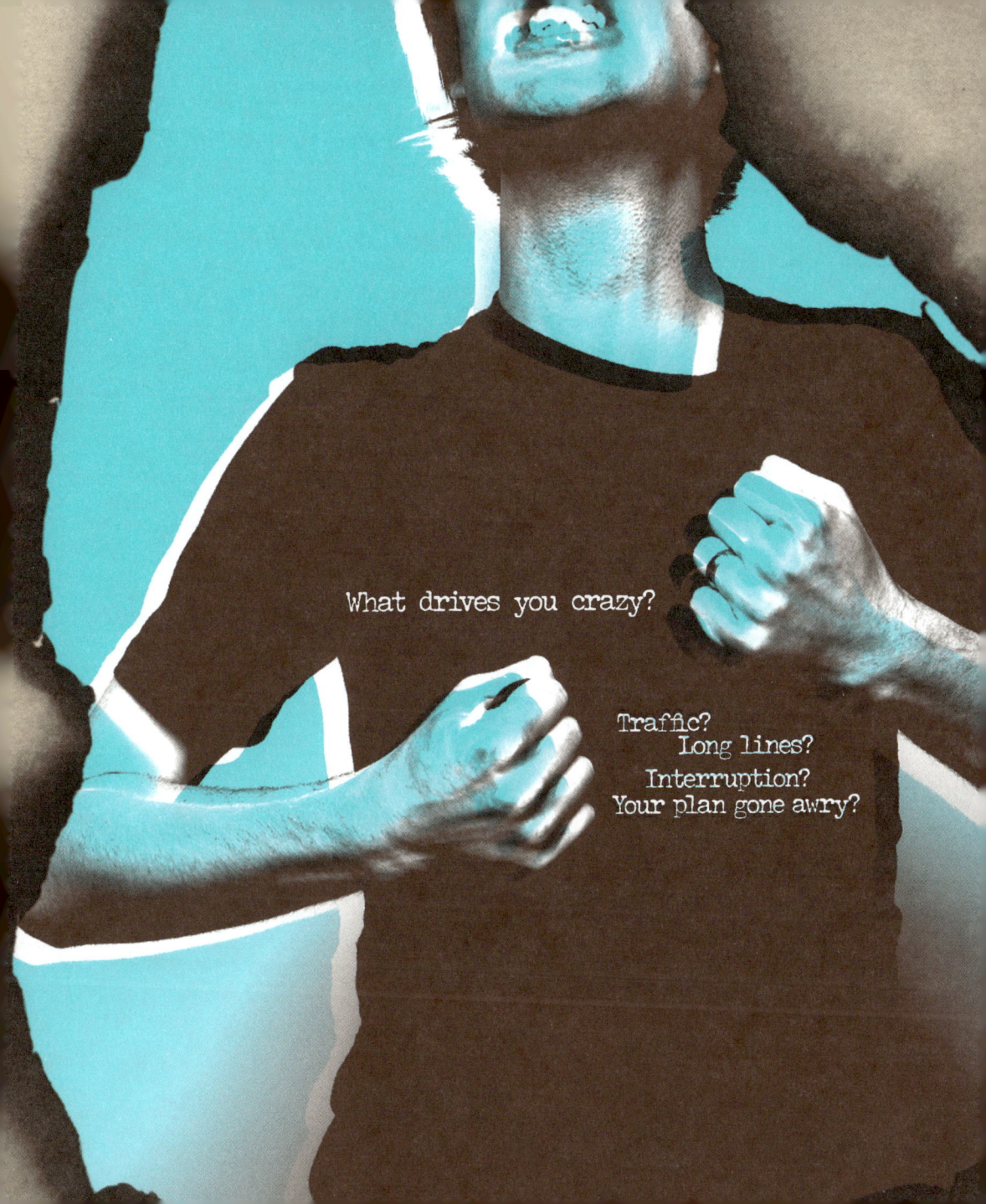

Do you think of God as being emotional? Is it easier for you to think of God as happy or as angry? Why?

As God's image-bearers, we will display a range of emotions similar to those experienced by God Himself. In our emotions we have the potential to bear God's image—but in our fallen state our emotions also have the potential to reveal the complexities and very specific flaws woven into the fabric of our stories.

Every emotion reveals an aspect of your spiritual DNA, your internal theology—the theology of the heart. What brings pain and thoughts of loss? Contempt, anger, sorrow, and joy reveal something about the "truth" your heart has adopted.

Behold, You desire truth in the innermost being,
And in the hidden part You will make me know wisdom.
(Psalm 51:6, NASB)

Recalling the man at the grocery store, what could his anger reveal about his core beliefs?
What might it reveal about his story?

God recognizes and wants to interact with our "truth"—what we believe in deepest places of who we are. This idea alone suggests that, for many, if not all of us, there is typically a disparity between what we say we believe and what we really believe. The heart has its own rules and reacts to each situation in accordance with an entirely different system of understanding. So how do I decipher this system? The key is to understand that your behaviors are the truest indicators of what you truly believe. In these emotions the heart tips its hand.

What could your emotions reveal about what you believe in the deepest places, your innermost?

THE LOUNGE

Lounges are supposed to provide some measure of comfort. We typically think of a teacher's "lounge" as a retreat from the hustle and bustle of the day. A hotel lounge has a similar connotation as does the soon-to-be-extinct smoker's lounge. Usually the lounge is at least a little insulated. When you enter there's the obvious feeling that you've left one world and crossed into another, each with its own lines of demarcation. A lounge can also be a place where a person goes for a dose of numbing—an escape of sorts. It's a place for artificial romance. Hook-ups with a veneer of romance. It's a dark place where reality isn't actually real. The lounge invites you to step away from accountability and "enjoy" the feeling of being absent from life and vacant of self.

There is a passage in Isaiah (47:7) that addresses the lounge mentality. It begins, "You said,

I will be the mistress forever."

Why do you think a person would be willing to be a mistress forever?

Do you have a version of an emotional lounge in your life? What and where is it?

"So now hear this, lover of luxury, who sits securely, who says to herself: I, and no one else, will never be a widow or know the loss of children" (Isaiah 47:8, HCSB).

The verse above refers to a person seeking to avoid loss. Has the prospect of avoiding a painful situation ever had appeal to you? When? Describe it.

Later in Isaiah 47 it is revealed that, for this lover of luxury that lounges so securely, there will be pain.

Do you think there is any value to feelings of disorientation or pain? Explain.

When we're sick we want to get well. At the prospect of pain, we'd rather avoid it. In fact, pain avoidance is a billion dollar industry. When we hurt we want to be healed. When we're sad we want to be happy, and when we're frightened we look to be comforted. In short, it may be said that we seek shelter in the lounge.

Why do you think God might be opposed to our lounges and our attempts to self-nurture?

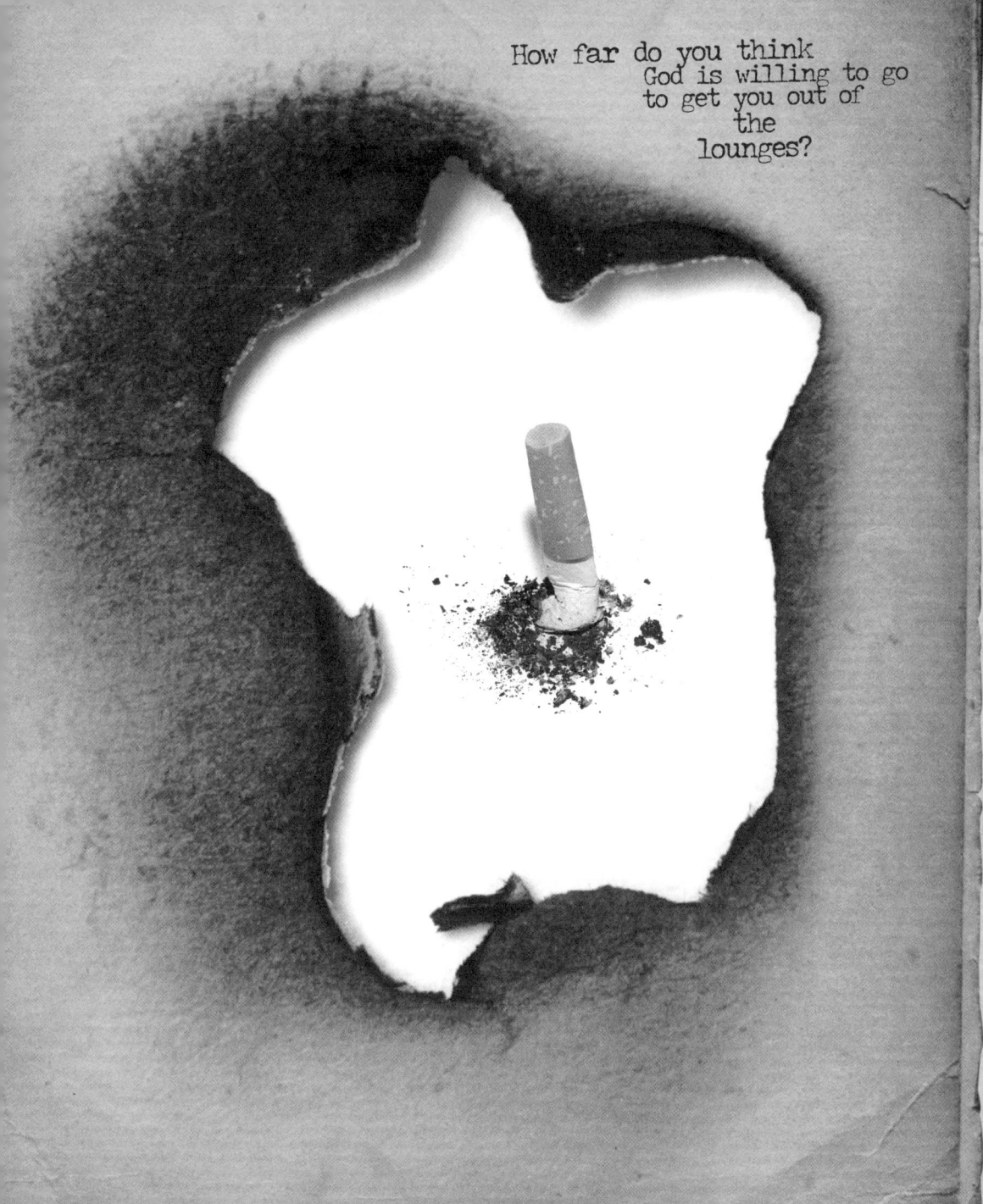

Conversation #4

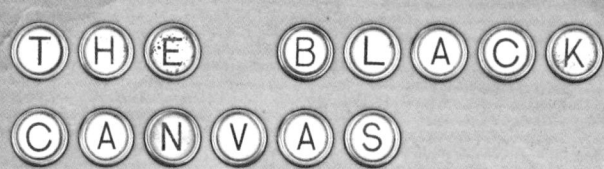
THE BLACK CANVAS

What smells,
sounds, and visuals
do you associate with a
city subway system? Metaphorically,
are there places deep inside you—inside
your story—you believe might be described similarly?

In the late 1970s when New York subway graffiti was just beginning to emerge as part of pop culture, Keith Haring was coming into his own style of art and self-expression. One day while riding the subway, Keith noticed something interesting about the advertisement posters along the subway walls: when an ad had expired, the agency would cover it with a soft, black, felt-type paper until another ad was purchased in its place—making it the perfect place for a piece of art. Keith darted off the subway train and quickly performed before a bustling public audience, hoping to finish before the police arrested him for vandalism.

Even though the chalk could easily be smudged or wiped off the canvas, those cartoon sketches were left alone for weeks and months at a time. Not because everyone knew who he was as an artist, but because of the social and political messages that pierced the onlookers. Keith was expressing his views, commenting on the issues of the day, and the people were listening. His art somehow struck a chord. The issues he dealt with were real—sometimes pretty raw.

What do you think is the difference between "real" and "raw"?
Keith Haring's art is described as "sometimes raw."
Why do you think raw art would be so compelling to people?

How honest is our culture?

What is it about rawness that strikes a chord in your soul?

Time to draw.
Express YOUR heart.

Spiritually, it's easy to remain underground. We may struggle with speaking about the times we think God had abandoned us. Maybe we dare not speak of the confusion in our lives that's caused by the senseless evil God has allowed to permeate this world. Perhaps we are shunned as shamefully faithless when we ask the big why questions.

So what do you think we're supposed to do with the less desirable sights, offensive smells, and frightening sounds that we might have locked deep within our hearts? Do you think God even wants us to ask?

What is innately beautiful about authenticity, rawness, and honesty?

He knows us inside and out, keeps in mind that we're made of mud. (Psalm 103:14, The Message)

Read Psalm 103:14. Do you think your heart at its rawest might be just as captivating to God as Kevin's art was to the people of New York City? Why or why not?

What do you think stands between most people and complete honesty with God?

As we live our lives submerged under the preconceived ideas of God that religions perpetuate—maybe even distort—how does the heart invite us to scribble outside the lines even just a little bit?

Conversation #5

BREAKING UP IS HARD TO DO

Do you think it's possible to love without experiencing a broken heart?

Why?

Which is easier to handle—getting publicly and totally rejected by someone whom you want to date and develop a relationship, or breaking up with that someone after four years of being together? Why?

Which phrase was uttered from your mouth when you first began that special relationship? "He's so hot!" "I can't quit thinking about her." "I can't believe he likes me." "I don't deserve her." These sentiments reveal the fresh fragrance of a newly blossoming relationship. It is the honeymoon, the spark, the beginning of a relationship when everything's good. It's the perfect picture. It's Eden. Remember how your heart soared. Remember how enthusiastically it leapt into the story. But on the other side you've probably experienced the extinguished spark; the death of the dream; or a relational springtime gone dry, cold, and stale.

Can you remember a romance that ended? How did you feel at the time?

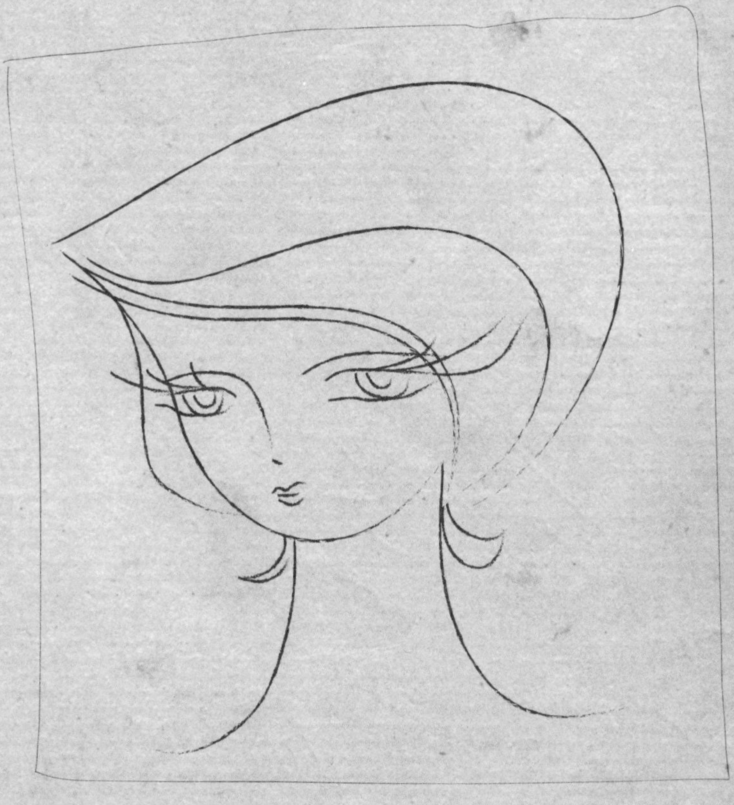

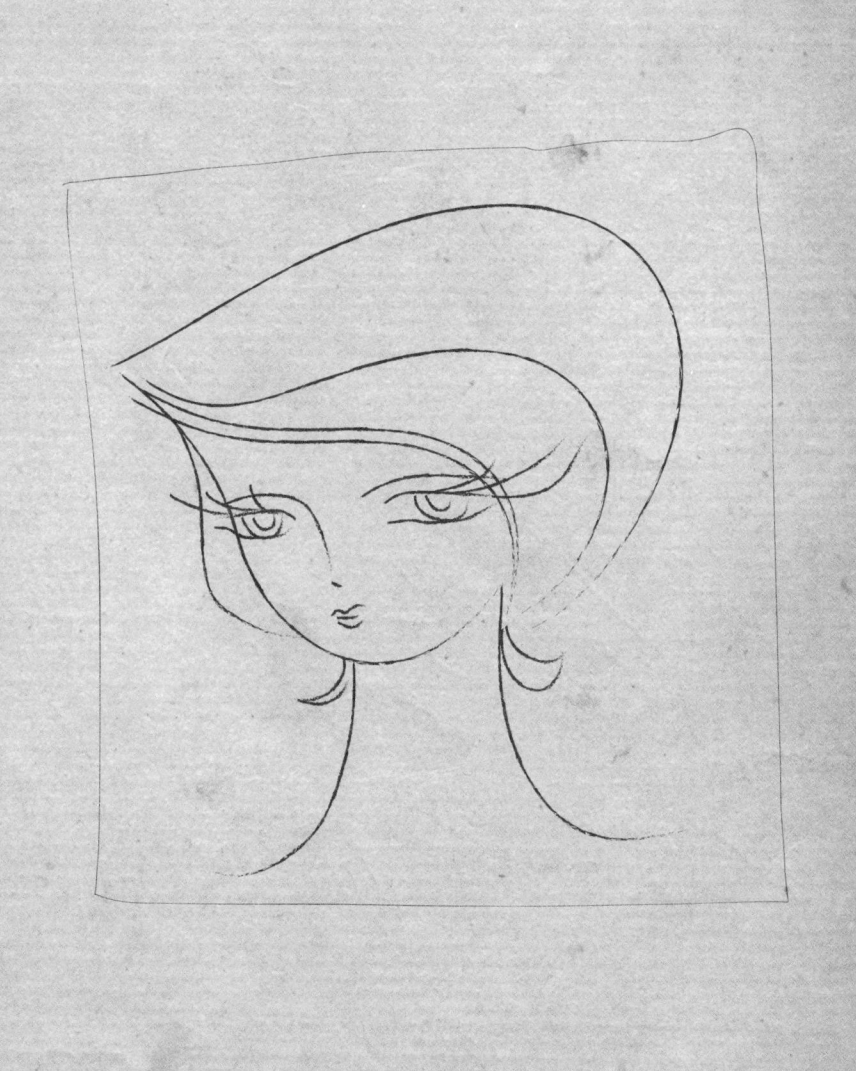

Everything's Good (day 6)
In Genesis chapter 1 the Scripture records six times that God's creation was good. On the sixth day after Adam and Eve were created, God even added a qualifier: "God saw all that he had made, and it was *very* good. And there was evening, and there was morning—the sixth day" (Genesis 1:31, NIV, emphasis added).

The Broken Heart
So the Lord God asked the woman, "What is this you have done?" (Genesis 3:13, HCSB).

Trying to Make It Work
"We can understand someone dying for a person worth dying for, and we can understand how someone good and noble could inspire us to selfless sacrifice. But God put his love on the line for us by offering his Son in sacrificial death while we were of no use whatever to him" (Romans 5:7-8, The Message).

When our hearts speak and our feelings flow, they tell our story. But don't forget that God has a story, too. Although God doesn't change, He doesn't go unaffected by the events of the story.

Do you think God has experienced the emotions associated with being broken-hearted? If yes, then how would you describe God's emotional dynamic as He experiences broken-heartedness?

What does this say about you—His image-bearer—and your heart?

What does it say about God that His heart can be broken?

ABANDONED

Conversation #6

Describe a time when you thought you were lost.

Growing up in church, the last thing you would ever hear in a Bible-study lesson is God just might abandon you. Even more outlandish, that God *wants* to abandon you! Imagine sending a child to a Sunday morning Bible study and upon returning, the little one shows off a picture he colored to illustrate what he learned. The picture is shocking: the child between a rock and a hard place—dangling off the edge of a cliff with one hand—and God is nowhere to be found. "Look mommy," little Johnny says, "God totally left me hanging!"

We would never teach something like that because it goes against the grain of our image of this loving, caring, ever-present, heavenly Father. We've read the Scriptures that God would never leave or abandon His children. Other passages reassure us of the concept that if God is for us, then who can be against us? And who can forget the promise from God that no one can snatch us out of His hands?

Even with those thoughts in mind, there are those times when God chooses to leave us alone. Of course it's not full-blown reckless abandonment, rather that He has chosen to leave us alone. Maybe He knows that we need to find desperation; that maybe there could be a redemptive despair.

Talk about the difference between God as silent and the prospect of Him as being absent.

Out of deep emotional distress (aka desperation), the heart will often make "I'll never" vows. These vows are powerful statements. Out of betrayal we might vow, "I'll never allow anyone to be close." Out of abandonment might come, "I'll ever need anyone." With each vow, trust grows thinner, what is truest about us grows more faint, and a part of our hearts shuts down. And your heart is the keeper of this part of your story every bit as much as any other part.

Do you think these vows are healthy? Do they serve a purpose? If so, for how long?

Do these vows need to be demolished or renounced? If so, why?

What do you think is the most effective way to destroy the "I'll never" vows? Do you think it's possible to un-do them?

King David experienced what he thought was abandonment by God. Here in the Psalms, David revealed his innermost emotions to God: "You don't let me sleep. I am too distressed even to pray! I think of the good old days, long since ended, when my nights were filled with joyful songs. I search my soul and think about the difference now. Has the Lord rejected me forever?" (Psalm 77:4-7, NLT).

Why do you think God would allow David to struggle like this?

In what ways do you think the sort of despair described in the Psalms above could be a good thing?

¹Some time later, Jesus went up to Jerusalem for a feast of the Jews. ²Now there is in Jerusalem near the Sheep Gate a pool, which in Aramaic is called Bethesda and which is surrounded by five covered colonnades. ³Here a great number of disabled people used to lie—⁴the blind, the lame, the paralyzed. ⁵One who was there had been an invalid for thirty-eight years. ⁶When Jesus saw him lying there and learned that he had been in this condition for a long time, he asked him, "Do you want to get well?" (John 5:1-6, NIV).

Why do you think Jesus would ask a man that's been an invalid—paralyzed—for 38 years, "Do you want to get well?" Doesn't this seem insulting? What do you think Jesus was really asking?

How do you think this man could have found comfort in his despair? What risks are associated with hope and healing?

What vows might have the paralytic described in John 5 have made?

Can the pain of despair awaken us to the possibility that there is "something more"? How do you think despair could actually work to revive the heart?

What vows have you made?

Use the abandoned area on pages 40 & 41 to capture the vows you may have taken and what you think God wants to say about them.

Conversation #7

BRAVO!

So there are several areas where everyday relationships produce the desire to want to please another person. But what happens when that healthy desire becomes an unhealthy obsession?

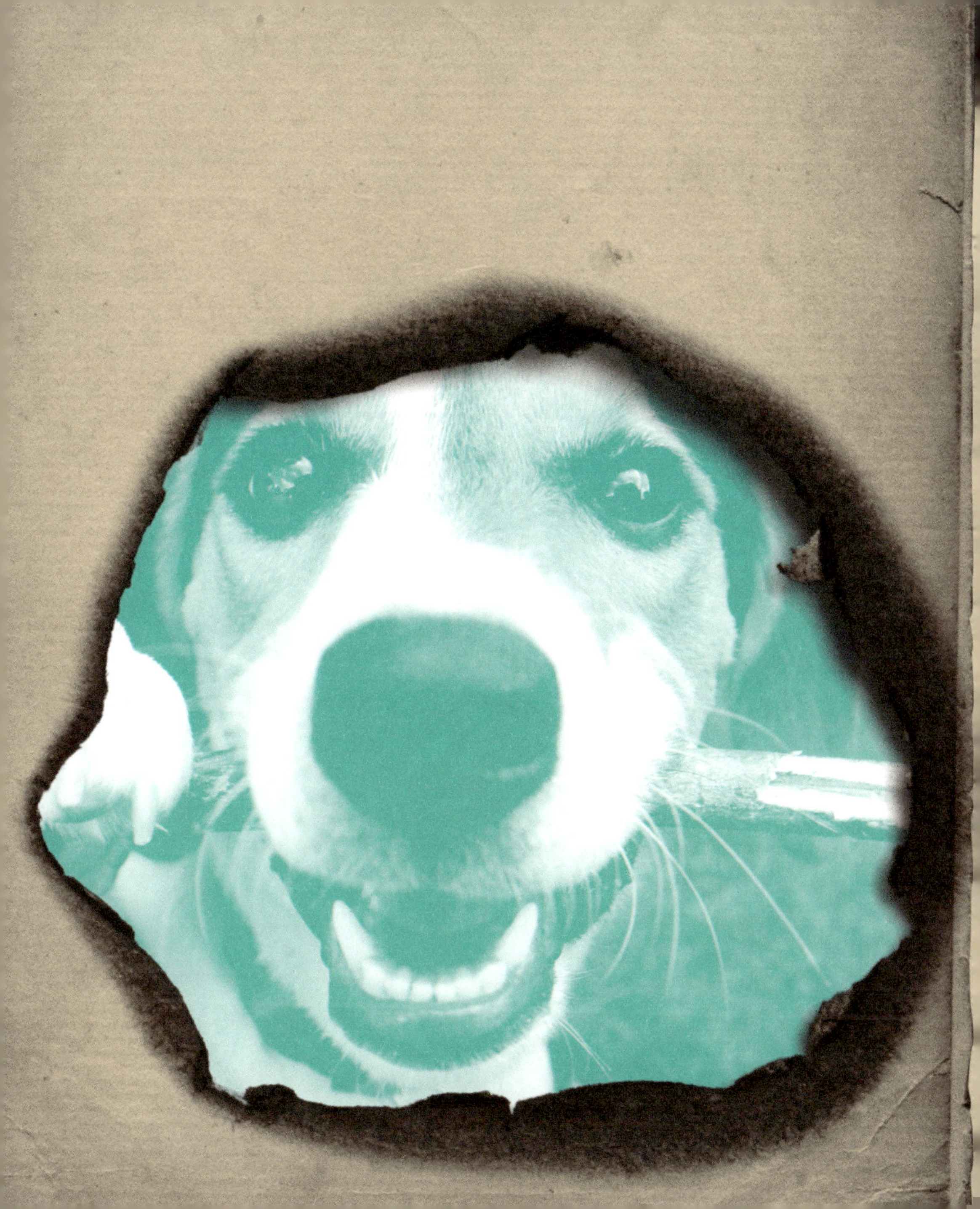

What could make someone believe he had to get everything absolutely, perfectly right?

_____

_____

What vows do you think might lead to a mistake-free obsession?

_____

_____

What could perfectionism indicate about a person's core beliefs?

_____

_____

When you first read about the adventurous journeys of Paul, the writer of a great deal of the New Testament, you must have thought, "Wow, what super-duper, awesome swashbuckler this guy is! He's always on a quest for Christ. He faces danger with the coolness of 007. His escapades take him on a venture across the known Mediterranean world! He must be a rock-solid super-human!"

Well actually, before Paul became the New Testament writer we know from the Bible, he was a committed people-pleaser. And he admits it, too. In Galatians 1, when he was ferociously defending the one true gospel, he told on himself. Paul said, "If I were still trying to please people, I would not be a slave of Christ" (Galatians 1:10). Apparently there was a time, at least according to Paul, when he lived at the mercy of the approval of others. This sort of affirmation dictated his every move.

Do you think God was disappointed in the people-pleasing Paul? Why do you think God chose Paul for one of His most vital missions?

Maybe Paul couldn't help it. Given his pedigree and pursuit of righteousness apart from God, he was very vulnerable to the opinions of others. Listen to him make the case for self-confident works: "Yet I could have confidence in myself if anyone could. ... having been born into a pure-blooded Jewish family that is a branch of the tribe of Benjamin. So I am a real Jew if there ever was one! What's more, I was a member of the Pharisees, who demand the strictest obedience to the Jewish law. And zealous? Yes, in fact, I harshly persecuted the church. And I obeyed the Jewish law so carefully that I was never accused of any fault" (Philippians 3:4-6, NLT).

According to Philippians 3:4-6, how would you describe the core beliefs of the people-pleasing Paul?

Survey your own compulsions. "I've absolutely got to _____"
(what)
What do you think your heart might be telling you through these obsessions?

Galatians 5:1 tells us that Jesus came so that we may be set free. Ultimately, freedom from these compulsions is at the very heart of Jesus' earthly mission.

DR. SEUSS, THE GRINCH AND INFINITY

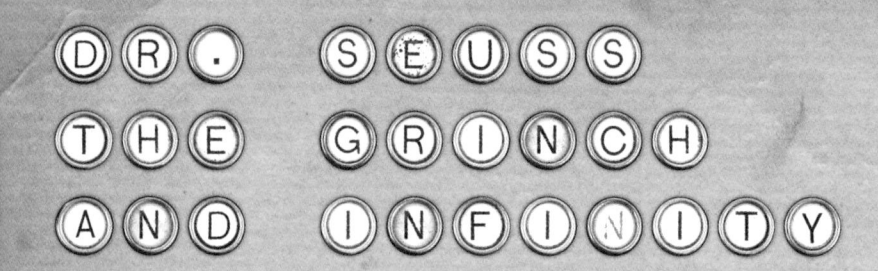

If you gained access to an emotional x-ray machine, what areas would you be willing to share?

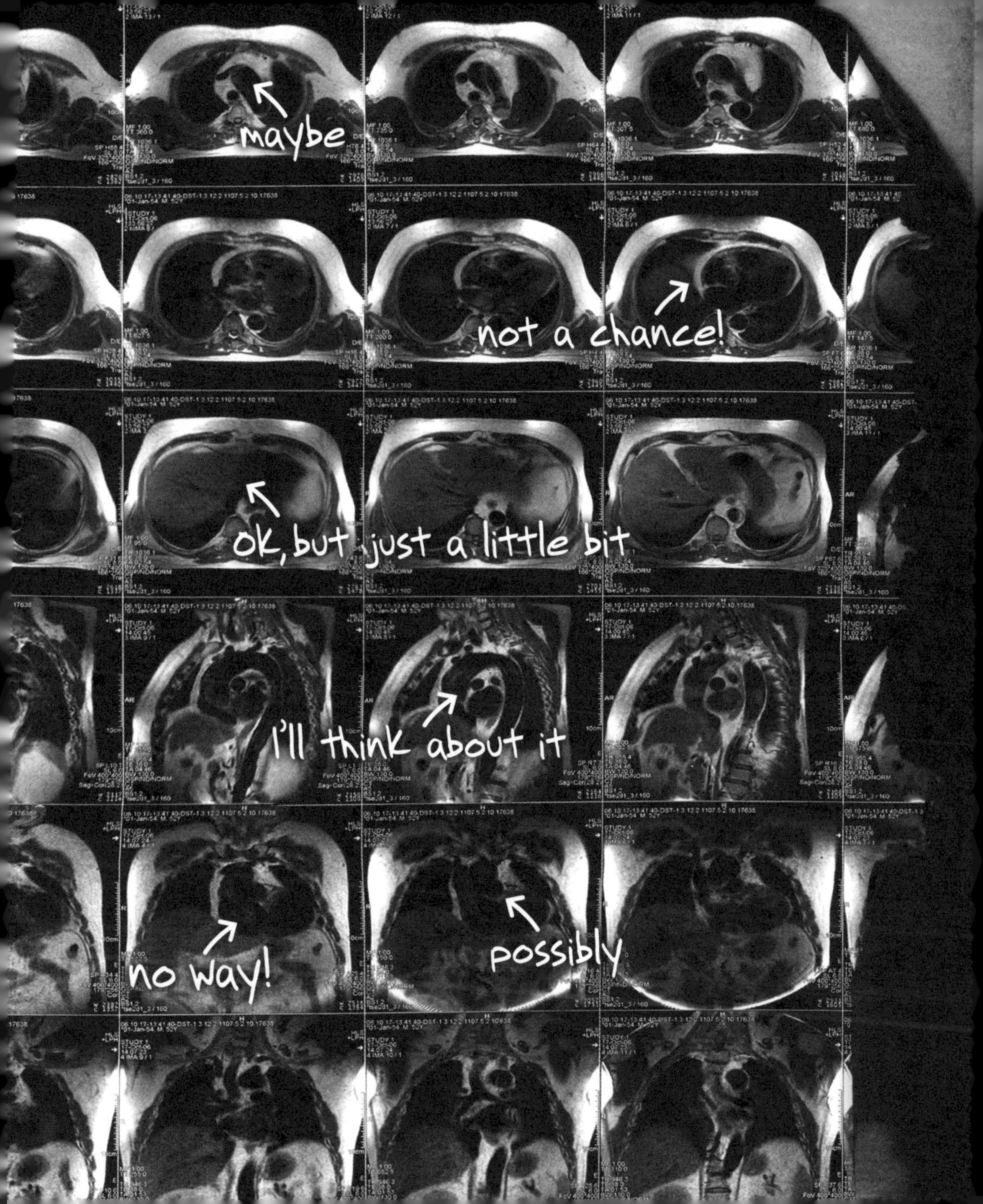
maybe
not a chance!
ok, but just a little bit
I'll think about it
no way!
possibly

If we took the character song from the movie *How The Grinch Stole Christmas* at face value, the Grinch would have to be one of the most disgusting, repulsive characters ever imagined. He's a mean one, a monster, a vile one, a foul one, and a rotter. His heart is an empty hole, full of unwashed socks, and a moldy, rotten tomato. He's got termites in his smile, and his soul is full of gunk. He is the king of sinful sots [translation: the Grinch is the biggest drunk known to man].

What do you think could possibly make a heart "two sizes too small"?

How do we know all this about the Grinch? Actually, it is very easy. If you watch the movie, you know that the Grinch's heart was miniscule. We get to see his heart on the magic x-ray machine and it reveals a heart that, very measurably, is two sizes too small. What is even cooler than this is later, through the magic x-ray machine, you actually see the Grinch's heart grow in huge proportion to the size it needs to be.

The Grinch's transformation is miraculous—and internal. His past circumstances are healed. But of course, as we've all come to learn, practically everything is possible in the Seuss-ian cartoon world.

If you had an emotional x-ray machine, what do you think you would see in our hearts as we are healed by God?

An IQ score is one of the ways we measure intellect. Our hearts have an IQ as well—an emotional IQ. The difference in the two IQs is that every heart has a maximum IQ score in a category best described as "emotional awareness."

³¹"The time is coming," declares the Lord, "when ³³...I will put my law in their minds and write it on their hearts."
(Jeremiah 31:31,33, NIV).

I will give you a new heart and put a new spirit in you.
(Ezekiel 36:26, NIV)

Therefore, if anyone is in Christ, he is a new creation; the old has gone, the new has come! (2 Corinthians 5:17, NIV)

According to the passages above, what has God done about our heart condition?

What happens to the heart condition of those that have a transformational encounter with Him?

The Grinch had an incidental encounter that collided with his internal world. This collision sent him on the way to transformation. Until that moment he had managed to avoid confronting a two-sizes too small heart while numbing himself through various means.

Do you think that your heart could be aware of things that your intellectual—more logical—side is unaware? Explain.

What are the consequences of avoiding an internal emotional confrontation with the heart? How do you think such avoidance can have effects "from this point forward"?

EARLY WARNING!

Conversation #9

On May 3, 1999, multiple supercell thunderstorms produced the largest damaging tornadoes ever recorded by radar. Forty people died in Oklahoma alone due to the twisters, and 675 were injured. Homes were demolished, businesses were destroyed, and lives were lost as seventy different tornados touched down to reek havoc in the heartland of America. One tornado in particular, the large F-5 tornado, reached a top speed of 318 mph—which only put it one mph below the wind speed associated with an F-6 tornado.

A tornado of that size is so inconceivable that, as it was actually occurring, the National Weather Service issued a warning they had never posted before. It wasn't just a Tornado Warning; it was a Tornado **Emergency** Warning.

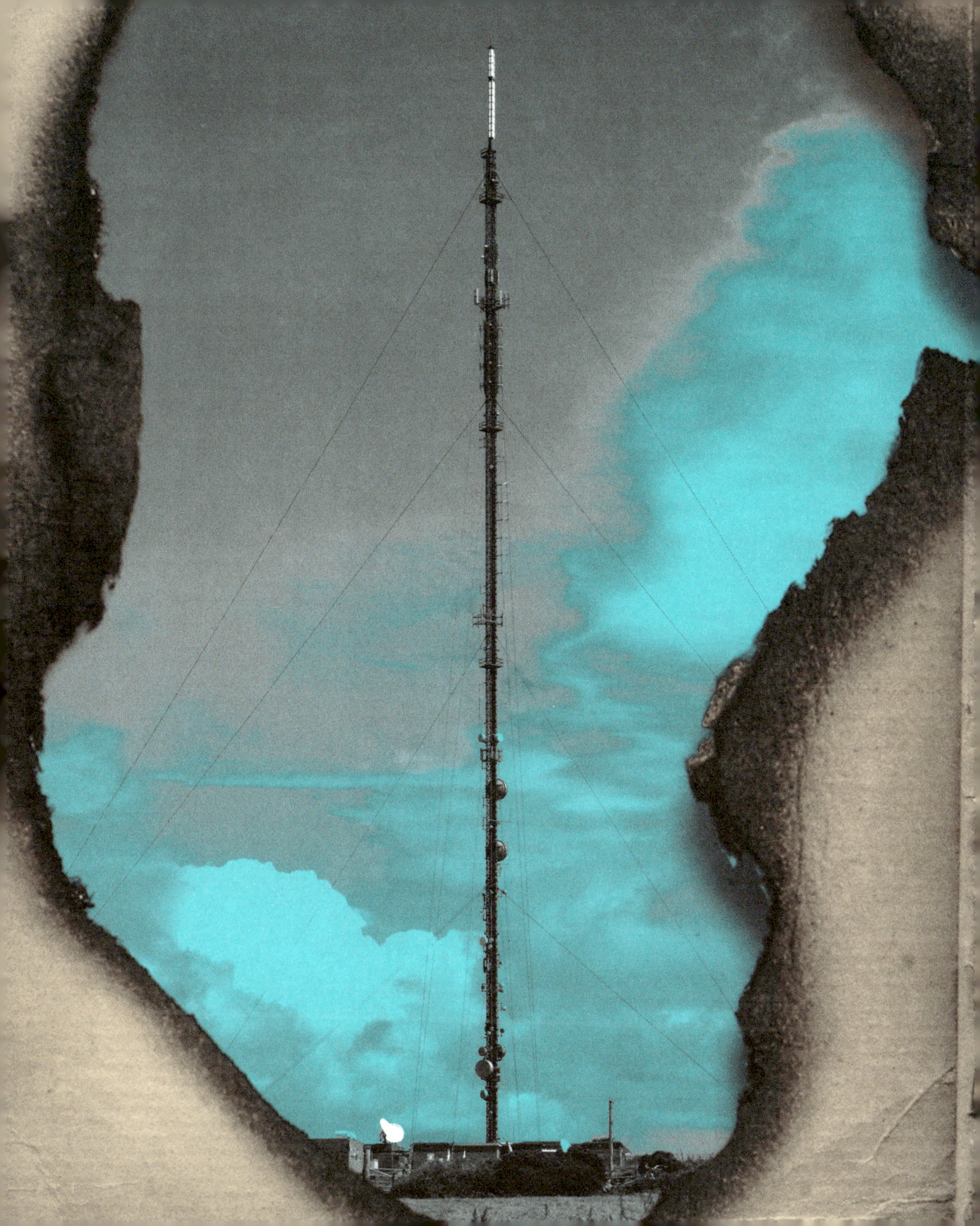

Describe a time when your heart sent out something like the Tornado Emergency Warning mentioned earlier.

Safety tips and precautionary measures for tornadoes and tornado warnings are drilled into school-age children across the nation. What drills have become commonplace for you in protecting your heart during Emergency Warning situations?

How does your story—memories, trauma, loss, reward, victory—affect your heart's ability to function as an early warning device?

Have you ever experienced a false alarm? What typically has caused the false alarms in your life?

When you think about the fears you have, what do you think your *Heart* may be seeking to protect itself from?

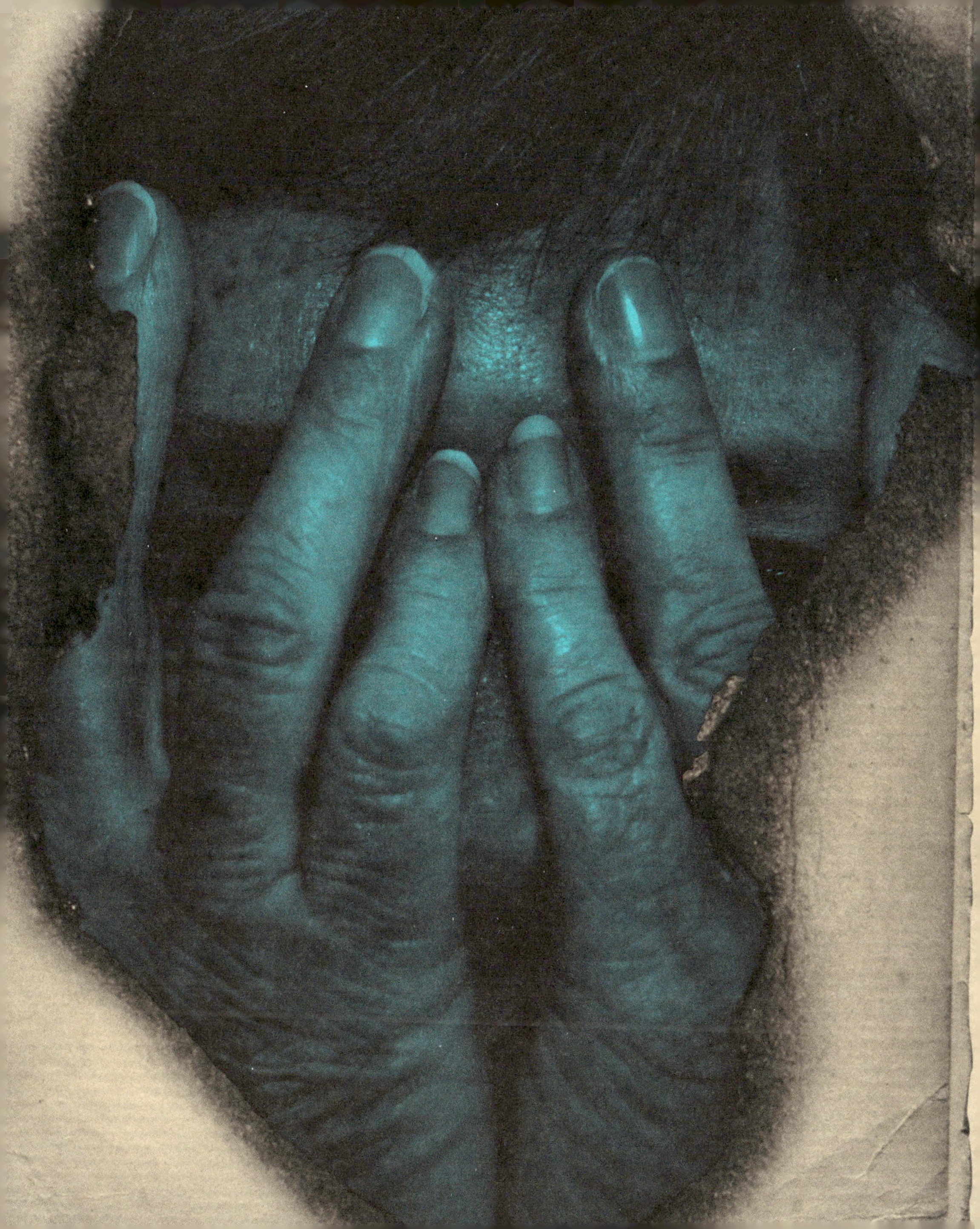

A Story about Jesus ...

Then he got in the boat, his disciples with him. The next thing they knew, they were in a severe storm. Waves were crashing into the boat—and he was sound asleep! They roused him, leading, "Master, save us! We're going down!" Jesus reprimanded them. "Why are you such cowards, such faint-hearts?" Then he stood up and told the wind to be silent, the sea to quiet down: "Silence!" The sea became smooth as glass. (Matthew 8:23-26, The Message).

Have you ever felt like Jesus was sleeping during one of your emergencies? How do you feel about a sleeping God?

Is it possible that the fear we experience is a symptom of a deeper, more intimate issue of the heart? The good thing about tornadoes is that they tend to be seasonal, temporary, and even detectable with the right technology. Can the same be said about our fear?

What do you think is the origin of fear? Is it sinful? If so, under what circumstances?

God allows fear because it can be helpful as an early warning. But like so many other things, fear has been distorted.

What sort of emotional journey does your fear normally take you on? What are the consequences of a fear that is allowed to progress unimpeded?

THE LINE

Conversation #10

What sort of things do you think **anger God?**

On June 25, 1993, an interview with music legend Johnny Cash was published by the Academy of Achievement entitled *"Music's Man in Black."* The interviewer asked Cash if there was any particular person that was important to him as a kid. Cash replied with, "In my little world, ... it was my brother, Jack. He was two years older than I and he was killed at the age of 14. He was a strong person, he was a Bible student, he was in perfect shape, physically. I always wanted to be like him."

Twelve years after this interview, the movie *Walk the Line*—based on Cash's autobiography—suggests that young Johnny Cash believed that God had taken the wrong son. And this belief, it seems, colored the remainder of Cash's life.

Why do you think Johnny Cash would have believed that God had taken the wrong son? From where do you think this conclusion would have come?

The truth is, this is not just about Johnny Cash. This is about us. A very big part of our spiritual formation stems from conclusions not entirely unlike those described above. Like a soldier dropped onto the beaches of Normandy, we are born into a world we don't understand, a world attacking from all sides. Our heart takes shots from all sides; some are fairly inconsequential, but some of these shots find our softest spots. The message, "You're not nearly good enough. That should have been you," clearly found its mark with Cash.

Talk about some of the hits that have found the mark in your life. Also talk about some of the messages that you have managed to defeat along the way.

What conclusions do you think you've made as the result of these wounds?

What role do you think our hearts play as we navigate the "beaches" of our own stories?

Jeremiah 6:13-14 reveals a little bit about what makes God angry. This passage tells us,
"From the least to the greatest … they are all frauds. They offer superficial treatments for my people's mortal wound. They give assurances of peace when there is no peace" (NLT).
Another version describes this sort of treatment as if applying band-aids to a mortal wound.

What does this say about how God values your wounds, your story, and the things you've come to believe? What does this say about how He feels about your heart?

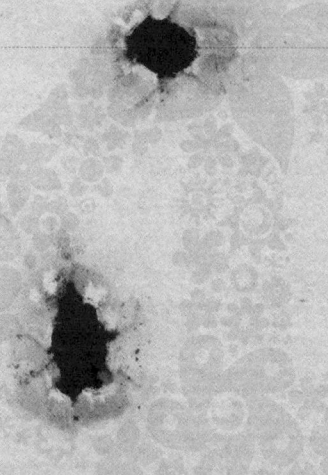

Other great small-group experiences from Serendipity House...

CANVAS
A DVD-driven small-group experience.

Emerging inside each of us is a unique work of art that reveals who we are and our vital role in the Larger Story. *Canvas* has been created to draw from deep within the stories God has given each of us, and to expose the beauty God is forging from the sum of our experiences. *Canvas* provides the context, the texture, and the materials for the journey. Through your story, your experiences, and the colors of your reality, God works to bring your role in the Larger Story to light.

Canvas: Distortions DVD Kit | 9781574943368
Canvas: Distortions Experience Guide | 9781574943375
Canvas: Mystery DVD Kit | 9781574944174
Canvas: Mystery Experience Guide | 9781574944181

GOD AND THE ARTS
Where faith intersects life.

Stories, great and small, share the same essential structure because every story we tell borrows its power from a Larger Story. What we sense stirring within is a heart that is made for a place in the Larger Story. It is no accident that great movies include a hero, a villain, a betrayal, a battle to fight, a romance, and a beauty to rescue. It is the Epic story and it is truer than anything we know. Adventure awaits. Look closer.

Finding Jesus in the Movies | 9781574943559
Finding Redemption in the Movies | 9781574943429

www.SerendipityHouse.com · 800.525.9563